How To  ...ess
For What It's Really Worth

NO-NONSENSE SECRETS FROM A
FORENSIC ACCOUNTANT AND CFO

To Andy,

Gerry T. Pandaleon, CPA, CMA, FCPA

*Thank you for being
one of my first clients.*

GOLDEN ALLEY PRESS
EMMAUS, PENNSYLVANIA

Gerry

G. Pandaleon/Golden Alley Press
37 S. 6th Street
Emmaus, Pennsylvania 18049

www.ForWhatItsReallyWorth.com

How to Sell a Business For What It's Really Worth/Gerry Pandaleon. –1st ed.
ISBN 978-0-9895265-0-0

This book is dedicated . . .
To my husband, Rob Pandaleon – my #1 fan. And to my children, Matt and Jackie, who always believed in Mom.
To Nancy Sayre, my editor, publisher, ghost writer, magician, and friend who has taken my words and ideas and created a work of art.
To Michael Sayre, book and 'Dance of the Deal' designer, my creative fan that allowed the book to take flight.

Contents

Appendix

Acknowledgements

There are four business individuals who influenced my career.

Mr. Harold A. Eisenhauer, CPA, gave me a foundation in accounting and taught me confidence. The late Mr. Gene W. Fickes taught me about manufacturing, and Mr. Scot Fickes first took a chance on me as his controller. The late Mr. Kenneth A. Longacre taught me about manufacturing, business deals, and business people. I am grateful for the significant role each of these men played in my development both as an accountant and as a person.

Portions of this book appeared, in article form, in the weekly journal Lehigh Valley Business.

Introduction

Even in a difficult economy, businesses are being bought and sold every day. Of those deals, the best ones are win-win for both parties. I want to prepare you for that kind of deal.

As the seller, you are focused on two things: getting the highest return possible and knowing you are conveying a sustainable company.

That is why I wrote this book. I want to teach you how to quickly build in as much equity as possible, avoid common pitfalls, and build a healthier company along the way. Selling a business can be very stressful; I want you to have as few surprises as possible.

Whether you own a small business (under $1 million in sales) or a mid-sized corporation (sales as high as $100 million), the process is similar. As long as you're not a publicly traded company, these principles will be useful to you.

If your business is struggling, and you're wavering between closing it and selling it at a fire-sale price, this book is for you, too. I hate to see businesses fail, especially if they were shuttered needlessly when they could have been turned around with some foresight and friendly advice. Your business may have more value than you think. Read on for encouraging ideas.

No matter what your reason for selling, my wish for you is that you walk away from closing with a nice fat check in your pocket, and the satisfaction of having followed a sound plan that allowed you to get the most out of your business investment.

This book is written in conversational language. I explain each subject deeply enough to give you actionable information, without overwhelming you with details. It is designed to be read two ways.

First, read it straight through from beginning to end. In the hour or two it takes you, you will gain a crash course in Business Management 101. If you are like most business owners, you will twinge a bit when you encounter areas in which you are weak. Make a note of those twinges—they represent money in the bank for you, showing you places you can build more equity.

Then, re-read the book with a notebook at hand. Organize your thoughts, create a timeline, and follow the Plan-Organize-Control-Feedback loop explained in Chapter 8. Now you have a plan which, if worked faithfully, will reward you both financially and with peace of mind.

I love to hear your business stories. Please send them to me:

Gerry Pandaleon
Owner/Principal
Continuous Financial Improvement
847 Wahneta St., Allentown, PA 18109
gerryp@ForWhatItsReallyWorth.com

[1]

Let the Selling Begin

OUR JOURNEY TO the settlement table has to start somewhere, so it might as well be at the beginning. Let's assume that you woke up just this morning with the determination to sell your privately-held business.

Until now, you've been busy making payroll and keeping your customers and suppliers happy. You've made no preparations for sale yet, but you're ready to hand the reins over to someone else.

Picturing a retirement villa in Palm Beach, you wonder, "What's my business worth?" You call your accountant, asking for a copy of your current business valuation. Can he help you sell your business? After first admitting that his firm only does taxes and estates, he excuses himself to run to the bookstore, where he snaps up all the "how to sell a business" books that he can find.

A tiny alarm goes off in your head; you decide it would be wise to educate yourself, and quickly. You grab a copy of *How to Sell a Business for What It's Really Worth* and settle in with a cup of coffee.

You take a look at your business valuation, and it gets you thinking. (If you don't have a current business valuation, go ahead and find out what your business is worth today. An informal valuation is probably sufficient for now. It will be the first of several business valuations that you'll need before your company is sold. More about that later.)

If you are pleasantly surprised by the business valuation numbers, good for you. But if your reaction is, "What? Is that all my business is worth?" your next question should be, "What can I do about it?"

THE GIFT OF TIME

Here is what you can do: tell yourself that you will sell your business in five years. Don't have five years? OK, three. Not even three? Then keep reading for ideas that will help your balance sheet benefit the most in the least amount of time.

If you accept that it will take some time to improve your balance sheet and income statement, you are off to a good start. Ocean liners aren't turned on a dime, and neither will your business. But even a little turning can yield great results. Imagine how the Titanic story could have ended, if only they'd had more agile steering.

Another reason to give yourself time to prepare for sale: prospective buyers want to see good five-year trends. Your job is to make the next five years show a good-looking trend of profitability. And since few people want to buy a business that isn't going to be here in the future, it must also pass the sustainability test.

THREE KINDS OF BUSINESSES: SOME TOUGH LOVE

In my practice, I have come across three kinds of businesses.

First, if you have a business that never makes a profit, it's really a hobby.

Second, you may be a 'lifestyle corporation.' You're in business to support your lifestyle, so you withdraw all profits either by salary, withdrawals, or dividend distributions. Each year you show either no profit at all, or a small loss.

For the third kind of business, you take a reasonable salary but reinvest back into your business and build equity into it.

If you are in the first or second type of business and want to sell it at a profit, it's time to change your attitude. Buyers are not interested in businesses that look like they are 'having trouble.' If they do want to purchase your company, it will be at a fire-sale price.

If you've been running a lifestyle corporation and have been taking all of the profit out of your business, the fix is fairly simple. Leave the profit in to buy new equipment, remodel the building, pay down your loans and build equity.

Sure, this will require you to take a cut in pay or dividends, or (gasp!) pay more taxes. But if you've been taking big bonuses for years, maybe it's time to cut the bonuses and reinvest in your company.

It will all be worth it in the end – when you get a better selling price.

A helpful interactive Business Selling Timeline is waiting for you at www.ForWhatItsReallyWorth.com.

[2]

Think Like a Buyer

"If you want to sell what John Smith buys,
See the world through John Smith's eyes."

THERE ARE LOTS of reasons you may be wanting to sell. Maybe you're a serial entrepreneur, ready for your next challenge. Maybe it's time to turn the business over to your children. Maybe you just want to start over, and start enjoying life again.

Whatever your motivation, the smartest thing you can do once you decide to sell your business is to start thinking like a buyer. So let's start there.

Curb Appeal

You've bought and sold a house before, so you know this intuitively: buyers look at property differently from sellers.

Home buyers want a picture-perfect house—no repairs, no roof leaks, no smells, no stains. Nothing to do but move in. If you want to compete with similar houses on the market, you'd better get to work—the sooner the better.

So you haul out clutter, repair leaky faucets, replace ugly floors, seal driveway cracks. And as you leave for settlement, you look around your spiffed-up house and mutter to yourself, "Why didn't I do this years ago?"

Business buyers are like homebuyers. They like curb appeal.

The dirty concrete, scruffy plantings, old computers and metal office cabinets that have worked fine for you won't fly for the new buyer. Prepare to spruce things up, inside and out, top to bottom. And your buyer will want perfect financials, humming machinery, pristine inventory neatly stacked in an immaculate warehouse, no debt, no musty receivables, a state-of-the-art website, and a world-class logo.

They'll have their team of lawyers and accountants crawling all over your financials looking for balanced accounts and up-to-date contracts.

You can be ready for them, if you start early. And there's a bonus in store. To do a good job preparing your business for sale means doing a good job of managing it in the meantime. It will gain equity, and may become such a well-oiled machine that you decide not to sell it.

Different Kinds of Buyers

Some extra savvy here will save you trouble in the long run. Different kinds of buyers have different hot-buttons, so make your best guess and be ready for your most likely prospect.

Buyers looking for a **long-term investment** will closely scrutinize both your balance sheet and your income statement. They are concerned with assets and the business's ability to generate income. Don't be surprised if the resale value of your business is also important to them. These buyers are often looking to 'buy a job' for their children.

Buyers looking for a **5-year flip** will, of course, want a payback of less than 5 years. They will be focused on the earnings multiple and the bottom line (profit) over the past five years, and want to see a five-year trend of increasing profitability.

Buyers looking for **a change in career** will be looking to replace their salary. Often Baby Boomers who have been downsized because their salary became too expensive to their employer, they probably come from a corporate environment and are somewhat naïve. This buyer is looking to buy himself a job and is usually in the desperate category. Regardless of what attracts him to your business, he will be interested in how he can gain control of his time. The longer he's been unemployed, the easier it will be to sell to him. To appeal to this type of buyer, get your business to the point that running it is 'job-sized'—so it nearly runs itself.

A buyer who has **a lawyer and an accountant looking on her behalf** will do a thorough job of due diligence. Your plant, records, and checkbook will all be scrutinized. The lawyer will check all legal documents; the accountant will check the value of inventory, machinery, and equipment and validate the existence of buildings, leases, and ownership. Accept that you must have everything 'just so.' Be prepared to engage in "The Dance of the Deal"; this is going to take some time.

For this buyer, it won't be an emotional decision. So your best bet is to use relationships to put yourself in an advantageous position. There is typically a lot of mistrust in the selling process, but you will be amazed at how much the magnifying glass is pulled back if the accountants and lawyers know and trust each other. Put your advocates' connections, networking and reputation to work for you.

A buyer who is **taking advice from an estate planner** will be particularly interested in the quality of investment he is making. Estate planners want to protect their client's money. If they are using some of their client's wealth (401K, pension, stocks, mutual funds, home equity loan, etc.) to buy this business, they'll want to be sure it's a very safe investment with long-term payback.

A buyer who is **a key employee in the business** will want to be sure that he can be in charge, that he can run the business the way he thinks it should be run. It represents his future. This buyer is usually a younger person, an employee who has worked his way up the ladder, such as the CEO selling to the CFO. He will be interested in longevity, so he'll want to improve things.

Since the CEO and CFO have mutual interests, these are usually very successful sales. The new owner's ideas can now be implemented, and he can be the final decision-maker. If you are in this situation, your best bet is to be as transparent as possible.

If the buyer is one or more of **your children**, and you are involved in succession planning, there are two key things to note:

1. Are they really interested? Disinterest is the hardest obstacle to overcome in the next generation. Be sure the business is in their heart, that they have the same passion and stomach for sacrifice that their parents or grandparents had.

2. Your business is probably in a different business cycle than it was when you started it. It takes a different personality to maintain a business than to start one, so your children need a different set of skills. This is why many second generation businesses fail. Don't make that mistake.

Tricks to Shift to a Buyer's Perspective

Is this your go-to-work-every-day story? You walk through the scuffed front door, past the dusty plastic houseplants, onto the brown indoor-outdoor carpet, sit at your putty-colored WWII surplus metal desk, and start your day.

That might seem normal, even frugal, to you; but to a buyer it will raise a red flag. Time to put on your 'buyer's glasses' and take the grand tour.

First, be an undercover customer at your store or facility. Walk through your warehouse. Pretend it's the first time you've ever been there—or send a close friend to do it for you. Make a purchase. Book an order. Search for a widget.

- What do you see, hear, and smell?
- What's the general vibe?
- What impresses you?
- What annoys you?
- How are you treated?
- How are the prices?
- Do the people seem pleasant and engaged?
- Is the facility clean and attractive?
- Would you want to shop there regularly?
- Would you want to work there?

Next, be a customer on your website. Pretend you've never seen it before.

- Does the design strike you as attractive?
- Can you find what you're looking for?
- Is it easy to navigate?
- Does it answer your questions?
- What pleases you?

- What frustrates you?
- Would you want to visit it often?

Now look at your financials with fresh eyes.

- Negative cash, large line of credit, big debt jump out at you? You may be used to looking at it, but a buyer won't be.
- Do you see a big bottom line? Are you thinking, "I could have fun with that?"
- Would you want to earn that amount of money?
- If there is personal stuff in your financials that won't apply to a new buyer (i.e. whole life insurance cash surrender value or a shareholder loan), take it out.

Next, change your attitude about paying taxes.

This is counterintuitive, but stick with me here. To build more value into your business, you will be wise to stop trying to pay the least amount of taxes possible. In fact, you may have to pay more income tax to build attractive equity into your business. This advice never makes me popular with my clients, but it works. The earlier you adjust, the better.

A health inspector once advised me that it's a good idea to visit the bathroom in every restaurant you frequent. If the bathroom is dirty, poorly maintained and in disrepair, the kitchen and financials are probably in a similar state.

[3]

Ready to Sell? Test Time

JUST BECAUSE YOU want to sell your business doesn't mean it's ready to be sold. Here are 16 sobering questions. Answer yes to all of them, and you're ready to roll. Answer yes to hardly any, and it's time to roll up your sleeves.

MOTIVATION MATTERS

First and foremost, identify your reasons for selling. Are your motivations healthy, or are you desperate? If you're not selling for the right reasons, you might be making poor decisions. And poor decisions now will eventually be reflected in what your buyer is willing to pay.

So examine your reasons for selling. Is it because of your health? The health of your business? For your pride? After too many years in the saddle, did you have trouble letting go, waited too long, and now you're running out of time? Be truthful.

Once you identify your motivations, grade yourself honestly on these questions:

1. Is your bottom line healthy?
2. Do you have a strong balance sheet?

3. Are your ratios good?
4. Is your debt low?
5. Are your building and machinery in good condition?
6. Is your inventory current, saleable, and pristine?
7. Is a strong management team in place?
8. Do you have sufficient employees / staff with proper skills and training?
9. Have you had a recent valuation done? Is the current selling price acceptable?
10. Is your technology up-to-date?
11. Are your website, branding, and marketing all working well and in harmony?
12. Are your accounting department and accounting software running smoothly?
13. Are all contracts with your customers and suppliers signed and updated?
14. Do you have current, signed contracts with all key employees?
15. Does your sales force have contracts with reasonable commissions?
16. Is your business stable and sustainable for the future?

Bonus question: Do you have clear, accessible documentation for all of the above?

If you answered YES to most of these questions, your business is probably in fine shape and ready to sell. Read on to answer your next question, "How do I know what it's worth?" Let's find ways to fine-tune and increase your equity.

If you answered NO to many of the questions, you have your work cut out for you. But this is no time to be discouraged and give up. First, read straight through to the end of the book. Then start again from the beginning, forming a plan to improve each weak area.

ONE QUESTION LEADS TO ANOTHER

By now you have even more questions running around in your mind. You are wondering:

Where do I start?
Where do I turn for help?
How long will it take to turn my business around?
How much will it cost me?

So let's get some answers.

WHERE DO I START?

Where you start depends on your endgame.

If you want the most money for your business, look at your current value, get an informal business valuation, decide what dollar value you want, then check with the professionals to find out what you can do to get from here to there, i.e. from $750,000 to $1,000,000.

If you are 55 years old and you realize you have 5 years to get your business where you want it, congratulations! You are reading this book at the best possible time. You want to improve your bottom line now, so you can show that great 5-year profitability trend that buyers want to see.

If you want to get out now, and want to do the quickest, cheapest things you can to gain the best value, get out the paint cans, reduce your debt, and maybe cut back on your paycheck.

If you haven't done a SWOT analysis (strength, weaknesses, opportunities and threats), start there.

In any case, make a plan and start executing it.

WHERE DO I TURN FOR HELP?

Help is everywhere, especially if you have the funds available to pay for professional advice. Once you've identified the weaknesses you are going to focus on, hire professionals in those areas.

When you're positioning your business for sale, your decisions will (and should) be different from 'the same old same old.' You need fresh ideas.

The first place to look is very close to home: your executive team. They often have ideas; they're just waiting to be asked. So ask.

If you don't want your exec team to know you're considering selling, perhaps you can tell them you're working on 'the improvement of the company' in general.

Next, look to your business advisors, lawyers, accountants, bankers, etc. Just make sure they have experience in buying and selling businesses—never just assume they do. There are great lawyers that know how to start a business, but know nothing about selling. And there are accountants that are good at taxes, but not at negotiating the sale of a business. To weed out unqualified candidates, use the helpful resource "12 Interview Questions to Ask Your Team of Professionals," available at the end of this book and as a downloadable PDF at www.ForWhatItsReallyWorth.com.

If your buyer is from a larger city, or more sophisticated and experienced at buying and selling businesses than you are, you may need to get a larger legal or accounting firm to represent you. You may need to go outside your comfortable circle of professionals—your buddy of 20 years may have served you well, but he or she may not have the experience you need now.

How Long Will it Take to Turn My Business Around?

Depending on the current condition of your business, it typically takes from 18 to 60 months to get a business ready for market.

Why such a long range of time? Buyers look at trends. If you've shown a loss for the last few years, it is going to take time to drop off the loss and show a profit trend. As a serial-entrepreneur friend of ours says, "One good year does not a trend make."

Like we said earlier, it's kind of like turning a ship. You need time to investigate why you have a loss, fix it, and show a consistently profitable bottom line.

How Much Will it Cost Me?

Of course the first answer here is: that depends. The second answer is: read Chapter 17. The third answer: here are a few rules of thumb.

If you already have a buyer, plan to pay some legal and accounting fees beyond the amount you normally pay annually.

It costs money to make sure you set the selling price for your business properly. You can simply stick a "For Sale" sign out and hope for the best, but our goal is to get the best price you can for your business.

We recommend doing it the right way, which means using audited financial statements and inventory. You can expect to pay anywhere from $20,000 to $40,000, depending on the amount of accountant and lawyer involvement. To keep this number under control, consider asking for a project fee instead of an hourly rate.

If you need to improve your premises and dress up your website and logo, get quotes and set aside money for those upgrades.

You know it's true: you have to spend money to make money. These investments will help your sale go smoothly and get you the best possible price.

[4]

Selling Price:
Book Value Plus Intangibles

IF YOU ARE LIKE most business owners, your accountant has been reporting the book value of your business to you for years. It's Accounting 101: assets minus liabilities equals equity (your net book value).

Accountants like this formula because it is based on historical cost. It's all objective; source documents prove the numbers. And don't fault them for their outlook. They answer to the IRS and GAAP (Generally Accepted Accounting Principles).

BOOK VALUE IS NOT YOUR FINAL ANSWER

But when you're selling your business, things are different. Everything is fair game—everything has a value.

You know that things like great customer service and keeping up with the latest trends in your business keep you profitable. But those things aren't reflected in your financial statements, and the numbers to prove that kind of value do not lie in your file drawers.

Now that you're selling, book value is only a starting point. Since the selling price is now all about how much your buyer is willing to pay, all of those intangibles suddenly matter very much.

Out With the Old, In With the New

These days, business valuations for selling a business are calculated in various ways: earnings multiples, net present value, market comps, discounted cash flows, etc. Traditional historical values are no longer 'in.'

Instead, your sales price will be influenced by the intangible worth of happy customers, a professional executive team, effective branding and marketing, desirability of the product, latest buying trends, predictions about the future, inventory, and processes.

Do buyers look at your historical figures? Yes.

Is the future outlook of your product more important than your financial statements alone? Yes again.

Tangible and Intangible

You will want to get the best value you can for both your tangible and intangible assets.

Your **tangible** assets, those that you can touch, feel, and see, will be appraised at market value. That is a (mostly) objective figure.

Your **intangible** assets, like the quality of your management team, the future growth of your product, the strength of your logo and branding, the effectiveness of your website, and networking relationships, will be given a subjective figure. These are the items that will really increase the worth of your business and put more money in your pocket at settlement time.

Broadly speaking, the selling price of your business is arrived at by combining your tangible and intangible assets (of course, the actual formula will be more complex). To arrive at those values, you need to go through the **business valuation** process.

In the next chapter, you will learn more about business valuations. First we'll discuss the importance of annual valuations. Then we'll walk you through the process step-by-step, teaching you what to expect. Loosely following the outline of your balance sheet and income statement, we'll show you where to make improvements that will give you the biggest dollar return for you effort.

Business Valuation: First Step to a Selling Price

I HEAR YOU THINKING, "Business valuations! What an expensive pain. I'll put that off until I absolutely have to."

Well . . . maybe.

Read on, and give me a chance to change your mind.

Your sense of dread probably comes from your impression of a *formal* business valuation. And you're right. It is complex, time-consuming, expensive, and generally optional.

But first, let's discuss the informal valuation. Then we'll tackle the more intimidating version.

INFORMAL VALUATION: A NEGLECTED REQUIREMENT

An informal valuation takes less time, less money, and fewer years off your life. It can be done by your own controller or CFO, managerial accountant, or business broker. The numbers are based on your own honest figures and are not audited, attested, or verified. It costs roughly 20% of the cost of a formal valuation.

Check your shareholder's agreement, partnership agreement, or buy-sell agreement. Chances are, it requires an annual informal business valuation. Nearly every lawyer puts it in the agreement. Nearly every business owner ignores it. But it's still a good idea.

True, you will probably only be held accountable to have one if someone dies or there's a divorce. It's kind of like an insurance policy that only gets read when you have a fire or theft.

Emergency or not, annual valuations are worthwhile. In my opinion, the accounting profession has done businesses a disservice in this area by not encouraging informal business valuations to be done often enough. True, it's risky for accountants to give an opinion, with all the rules, guidelines, and malpractice threats. Nevertheless, annual valuations are an incredibly valuable tool.

First, they are an important reality check. They help you pause from 'making the pies' to think about the future of your business. Is it worth all your blood, sweat and tears? Or is it time to sell? Without the discipline of an annual valuation, these important questions might not get asked.

Second, they help you avoid doing an emergency valuation if there is an unexpected death. Imagine this scenario: family members panic, wondering when the last evaluation was done. Was it ten or twenty years ago? The grieving family has enough to deal with following a death. So be wise and evaluate your business when everyone is calm and healthy.

Third, insurance companies often require an informal valuation when they provide a policy to fund your buy-sell agreement. A new trend is for them to do their own valuation. But I still recommend you get an outside opinion on the value of your business.

For selling purposes, business valuations contain clues for improvements you can make to increase your selling price or make the sale go more quickly.

For all of these reasons, I recommend that you obtain an independent informal or formal valuation, whichever your pocketbook can afford.

If you are one of those rare companies that actually does perform the annual valuation, congratulations. You already have a basic idea of what your business is worth. The person doing the valuation can tell you if they think the valuation price is also a good selling price.

I also want to mention the Opinion of Value Report (OVR), another way of estimating the value of your business. It is shorter, less expensive, and can be done quickly. You provide your unaudited numbers, an accountant loads it in a software package, and out comes a report.

An OVR is useful, but it isn't as effective in establishing a selling price.

FORMAL VALUATION: CHECK AND DOUBLE CHECK

A formal evaluation is more, well, formal. Its biggest advantage: your buyer will have much more confidence in your numbers because they have been audited, tested, examined, and generally scrutinized under a microscope.

A formal business valuation is best performed by a CVA (Certified Valuation Analyst), or by a CPA with an ABV (Accredited in Business Valuation) accreditation.

More than one person usually works through the information you submit. One team looks at assets and inventory. An appraiser validates the value of buildings, property, and assets. Auditors delve into your books to audit the income statement and verify the value of your inventory.

A formal valuation is indeed expensive—usually in the $20,000 to $40,000 range. Because virtually the same amount of work must be done, the number remains nearly constant whether you own a $1 million company or a $100 million company.

Even though a formal business valuation is expensive, I still recommend that you have one done before you set the selling price. Just be sure to prepare your business first, so you get the best value.

THE GOLF COURSE METHOD OF BUSINESS VALUATION

No matter what valuation method or approach you end up with on settlement day, it will all probably start off with a conversation about your annual income and what earnings multiple you used to arrive at a selling price. This is definitely not a precise method, but I want you to be prepared for these conversations when they occur.

Realistically, no one says, "I would like to have $934,128 for my business." More likely, you will be out on the golf course or in a restaurant. The conversation between you and your trusted business colleague will go something like this:

You: "Would you pay $1 mil for my business?"

Friend: "I don't know. What's your bottom line?"

You: "$250K."

Friend: "Sure, if I can get my money back in 4 years."

Owners are typically natural-born salespersons. So they (and that probably includes you) are going to test the water before they call in the professionals. Take a lesson from Andrew Carnegie (see story below). If he hadn't had a number ready to write down on a slip of paper in 1901, one of the most famous business transactions of all time might never have happened.

MORE ABOUT THE EARNINGS MULTIPLE METHOD OF VALUATION

As the business owner, your favorite way of arriving at a business sales price will probably be to multiply EBIT (Earnings Before Interest and Taxes) by your Earnings Multiple. For example, if your EBIT is $1 million, and you use an earnings multiple of 7, your business is worth $7 million. This method is quick and easy, especially if you use an earnings multiple you've grabbed off the Internet. But you should explore all methods before you set your price. (Earnings multiples can range from 1 to 12, depending on your type of business.)

Note that, if you use this method, EBIT becomes a vital determinant of how much your business is worth.

Instead of EBIT, some valuators use EBITDA (Earnings Before Interest, Taxes, Depreciation and Amortization). Obviously, if depreciation and amortization are excluded from earnings, this number will be greater than the EBIT number.

Understand which number is being used (EBIT or EBITDA) and expect discussions about it.

Be sure to recast your financial statements properly. It is important to normalize or remove income or deductions that your buyer will not experience.

To repeat, this is a method used to get the ball rolling, to select a dance partner for "The Dance of the Deal." Leave the final calculations and details to your lawyer and accountant. They will use the method that best fits your situation.

Not every business deal is made by way of formal valuations and accountant-proven numbers. In 1901, the largest business transaction of all time (adjusted for inflation) was undertaken because of a single number written with a stubby pencil after a day of golf. When J.P. Morgan's intermediary asked for Andrew Carnegie's price to sell Carnegie Steel, Carnegie jotted a number on a slip of paper. Without countering, Morgan accepted Carnegie's price of $400 million.

[6]

Preparing for Your Business Valuation

WHEN I DO an informal business valuation in preparation for a sale, I walk my clients through the steps outlined below. Your accountant's routine will probably be similar. I have included talking points along the way so you know what to expect.

The preliminary steps for a formal valuation are similar, but the timeframe is longer, and you will have the added layers of outside verification of all numbers.

INITIAL MEETING: BACKGROUND INFORMATION

Goal: to gather information so I can see the business as it really is.

· Determine the seller's motive for selling
· Determine the seller's goal for selling
· Determine the selling price the owner is hoping for. (Although it's my job to calculate what the business is worth, I always want to know what number is in my client's head. And they always do have a number in mind.)

- Ask questions concerning current and future management of the company. (For example, when you sell, do you plan to stay for the transition or head immediately to Florida?)
- Date and copy of most recent valuation
- Tax returns and financial statements for previous 5 years

SECOND MEETING: GETTING TO KNOW YOU

This time, we meet to discuss the current status of the company and predict the future. Yes, we try to predict the future.

The discussion of the current status of the company is always very interesting.

Often I have clients that have been in business for 30 years, yet never really understood their income statement and balance sheet. Their accountant just gave them their tax return in a hurry—"Just sign it and pay the taxes."

They admit it was their fault that they never learned to read the statements. They, too, just wanted to get out of the accountant's office ASAP each year.

So once I've explained the statements, and my clients completely understand their current status, then and only then can we talk about where the business will be in five years.

I ask: will the product continue to sell the same, less, or better? Are there economic factors or government rules that will help or hurt your business in the future?

I collect more details:

- **Type of business:** Sole Proprietor (Schedule C), Partnership, Corporation (1120 S, QS?)

- **Building and machinery:** If there are buildings that need to be appraised, I recommend an appraiser. If not, I use the current book value of plant assets. I need to know what year the value was put on the books.

- **Accounts receivable:** I obtain an aging report. For the buyer's benefit, will a notarized document be sufficient verification that AR is current and accurate?

  When I'm dealing with you as seller, I hope you are truthful about your accounts receivable. If you want a buyer to have more confidence in your numbers, you can have a list notarized to your statement of fact regarding accounts receivable and cash flow.

- **Inventory:** I obtain an inventory list, which a seller should have in the normal course of business. I tell them to throw away obsolete and damaged inventory before they even give me the list (see Chapter 9). We also consider notarizing the inventory list for the sake of our buyer.

- **Legal agreements:** I check for the following:
  Pending lawsuits or other legal deficiencies
  Employment agreements
  Building lease agreements
  Franchise agreements
  Any other contracts or agreements (Your lawyer will probably add more to the list)

- **Changes in the industry:**
  Laws that will increase or decrease income
  Laws that will increase or decrease expenses
  Inspection requirements

- **Business loans:** current bank agreements

- **Personal loans:** either receivable or payable, to be settled up prior to purchase date

- **Recast financial information:**

  One-time non-recurring expenses (i.e. legal expenses for the sale of the business)

  Excessive owner expenses: salary, meals and entertainment, vehicle expense, etc.

- **Management of the business:** list of key employees

- **Achievements in your field:** awards, etc.

Next, we evaluate your company (usually on a scale of 1-4, but any rating system can be used) in about 15 areas, including:

- **Industry growth** – stable or rapid growth

- **Business growth** – meets or outperforms others

- **Business financing** – only accepting cash deal, or open to seller financing

- **Competition** – many or few

- **Location** – desirable location or difficult access

- **Customer concentration** – many customers or few select customers

- **Product/service concentration** – many products or just a few products

- **Market** – local only, regional, national

- **Nature of your business** – easy to get into or high barrier to entry

- **Desirability** – is this a business many or few buyers will consider

- **Ease of operation** – turnkey or completely owner driven

- **Employees** – skilled or unskilled

- **Management** – executive team or owner only

- **Seller financing** - available, at what interest rate, not available

We spend more time discussing our predictions for the future. Then I input the data into spreadsheets, put on my futurist's hat, and predict the next five years. (This is why valuations are risky, and why many accountants avoid them like the plague.)

FINAL MEETING: RANGE OF VALUE

At our final meeting, I present the range of value of your business. Since it is difficult to pinpoint an exact value for your business I always look at its value using four different methods. Each method renders a different number, developing a range of values that your business is worth.

As an example, for a $1 million business, the numbers would range from $750,000 to $1,100,000, calculated something like this:
- Based on Earnings Multiple, your valuation is $1,100,000.
- Based on Discounted Cash Flow with a 2% growth rate, the valuation is $850,000.
- Based on Business Goodwill, the valuation is $900,000
- Based on Market Comps the valuation is $750,000.

My numbers will be based on information you provided to me, with no audit, verification, or attestation done to validate that number. This is why it is an informal valuation. We are merely setting the selling price. If the price you were hoping for falls within that range, we are good to post it for sale. If not, we start planning how to get there.

[7]

Line-by-Line Strategies to Increase Your Selling Price

THE FIRST THING to say about increasing your selling price is this: direct your efforts where they will have the most impact.

Improve the Most Leverageable Items First

Naturally enough, people will begin with your balance sheet and income statement to value your business.

To prepare for this, let's take a quick tour through the most leverageable of your tangible and intangible assets, roughly ordered as they appear on your financials. These are the places where you can build the most equity ASAP.

Your Balance Sheet: Assets

Why is your balance sheet so important to a buyer? Because it represents a snapshot, the value of your assets at a "point in time." So that is a major part of what the prospective buyer is buying. **Improvements here will add directly to the worth of your business.**

1. Cash – watch it closely.

This number seems self-evident, but there is more to it than meets the eye. This is just a number at a point in time. Cash is easy to understand, but harder to pin down.

Keep an eye on your cash number at the time you're negotiating and at the day of settlement. When you show a prospective buyer your balance sheet, they'll have a tendency to assume the cash figure is an average.

As a seller, be honest and share with your prospective buyer as to whether the number is an average or not. Don't play games with this number—it will only come back to bite you in the end.

2. Accounts receivable – are they current?

Clean up all accounts receivable over 30 days and keep it up-to-date. If you don't, the buyer will cross out all receivables over 30 days, immediately decreasing the value of your business.

3. Inventory – is it saleable and pristine?

Get rid of all old and damaged inventory. If you have valued it on your inventory list, you are only kidding yourself that you'll get full value for it.

At best, buyers will cross it out, decreasing your business's value. At worst, if you leave old or damaged inventory in your warehouse and the buyer sees damaged pallets, you could lose the sale entirely.

On the other hand, if your inventory is in great shape and valued properly, it can increase the value of your business.

For manufacturing and retail, especially, this is a significant percentage of your balance sheet. Pay close attention to Chapters 9 and 10 for more in-depth inventory advice.

4. Plant, Property and Equipment (PPE) – is it in good shape?

Starting from the outside, fix up your building. Make sure it is completely code-compliant, from fire, to handicap, to safety. Then get your building appraised. Don't get an appraisal first, then fix things up, or you'll have to pay for the appraisal twice.

Check your books. If you've owned the property for many years, PPE could be significantly below market value.

Keep looking at your property with a buyer's eye—so you notice things like the nicked-up, paint-peeling front door that you walk through every morning.

5. Intangible assets – buyers are always interested in patents, trademarks, and intellectual property.

Patents and intellectual property are valuable to your buyer only if they are producing current, profitable sales. If your patents and intellectual property are as valuable as you say they are, that will be the case. They will be an excellent bargaining chip if you are constructing an 'earn out' deal.

You and your buyer must both believe in the strength of your patents, trademarks, and intellectual property. Of course, the more recognizable your trademark is, the more valuable it is.

Make sure you have all the paperwork and documentation on your intangible assets, and that everything is up-to-date.

Because this is such a business-specific value, your own industry will dictate this value.

6. Other intangible assets – goodwill, branding, etc.

Improving an outdated or outgrown corporate image can give great ROI. If you're obviously due for a rebranding, the new buyer will mentally deduct that amount from the bottom line of your asking price.

On the other hand, if your branding is fresh and inviting it will add value to your selling price in the same way that spending $10,000 on improving your kitchen can add $50,000 to your home's worth. Better to do it now and start building brand equity.

Your Balance Sheet: Liabilities

The first thing to say about liabilities is that no one wants to take over your debt.

Think of it this way: less debt is more value. So make it your mission to get out of debt as quickly as you can. If you can't reduce your debt, make sure you have good interest rates and loan structures.

Your liabilities are divided into two sections: current and long-term liabilities.

Current (Short-Term) Liabilities

Your two most important current (or short-term) liabilities are accounts payable and your line of credit.

1. Accounts payable

The higher your accounts payable, the lower the value of your business.

Don't fall into the trap of using your accounts payable as your own little line of credit. That may have worked in the past, but you don't want to outsmart yourself now that you're a seller.

There is nothing worse for a prospective buyer to see than a fax saying, "If you don't pay your invoice, you won't get your delivery." You want to transfer a healthy vendor relationship to the new owners.

Keep your vendors happy. Pay them on time from this day forward.

2. Lines of credit and covenants

Read these documents closely and make sure you know their terms. There may be a line in a covenant that says you must notify the bank when you are planning to sell your business.

It's an excellent policy to pay your line of credit down to -o- at least once a year. Even if it's only one day, that proves you can pay it down.

Your buyer may want to assume your loan, so be sure it is truly used for inventory or working capital, not to buy a car or equipment.

LONG-TERM LIABILITIES

These are long-term commitments for large dollar items. They are usually secured with a car, van, truck, or large piece of machinery as collateral.

Time was, these loans only came from banks. Now it is common for manufacturing companies to offer loans. Some big-ticket items are financed by a combination of bank loans and equipment vendor loans.

If you've negotiated a really good deal, that is attractive to a buyer. Be sure to point it out. They might not have as good of a relationship with their own bank, and want to assume your loan.

Banks may require renegotiation, but most equipment vendors will allow your buyer to just assume the loan.

YOUR PROFIT STATEMENT

You may wonder why, if the balance sheet is so important, you have to show a good profit as well.

Here are two big reasons. First, your buyer will absolutely want to see a profit.

He wants to know if the profit can cover the debt of the business, and how long it will take to recoup the money he is investing. He wants to know whether he will get his money back through a healthy salary, or not until he, in turn, sells the business.

Second, showing a profit is important because it is used in the 'earnings multiple' method for valuing your business.

Remember, your financial statements tell a story. What story are they telling about your business? It is a smooth running company, or is the road a bit bumpy?

1. Income Statement Revenue (Sales) – tells whether or not you have customers.

These are some questions you should be able to answer:
- How many customers do you have?
- How often do they buy?
- Is the business seasonal?

Sad to say, I've encountered business owners who can't answer these questions. So do your homework ahead of time.

Don't be surprised if you are asked for non-financial as well as financial data here. Your CRP (customer service report) software will provide this.

2. Cost of Goods Sold

Be prepared to give unit cost and plant and labor efficiency information. These numbers, if good, can be great selling points.

3. Operating Expenses

Know and control your own big hitters in this area. Utilities? Rents? Make sure they are within control.

4. Selling Expenses

Know what percentage your business spends on advertising. Be prepared to show what advertising contracts you have signed. If they are long-term and not worthwhile, they can be a real problem, so take care of this now.

5. Salespeople and Contracts

Put yourself in your buyer's shoes and take a close look at your sales contracts.

Would a buyer agree with your commission structure, or is it in place simply because that's the way you've always done it? Are contracts too high? Too strict?

Watch out here—how commissions are structured can make or break a deal.

6. Administration – Your organization chart

Put your buyers' shoes on here again. Would they agree with your organizational structure?

Examine officer salaries. If they are too low, the buyer may want more salary. If they are too high, they may need to be reduced to allow more profit to flow to the bottom line.

Find out how your structure compares to similar businesses.

[8]

The Plan-Organize-Control-Feedback Loop

NOW THAT YOU'VE identified what areas of your business you need to work on, here is a solid method for making the changes that will increase your sales price.

Whether you learned this in your MBA courses or by the seat of your pants, you'll recognize the value in the Plan-Organize-Control-Feedback process. Make it your habit, and you'll reap great benefits.

Plan: to establish a 5-year positive balance sheet and income statement. Using Key Performance Indicators and the Plan-Organize-Control-Feedback loop, you'll make sure you are on track to achieve your goals.

Organize: your plant, people, and paperwork. If you run your company out of your shirt pocket, it's time to document your procedures. Write some SOPs. Buyers will sniff out disorganization in the way the front office answers the phone, how orders are manufactured and processed, filled, and delivered. You may have a great product, but if you can't conduct business in an organized way, it will show.

Control: A good, old-fashioned timeline is the best way to control a project of this scope. Also set limits for your goals. For example, if one of your goals is to maintain $100,000 in cash for the year, and you don't do it, it's not in control. (Make use of the "Business Selling Timeline" waiting for you at www.ForWhatItsReallyWorth.com.)

Feedback: Don't leave this step out, because feedback enables you to be flexible and realign according to economic and environmental changes occurring during the process. Learn how to use key performance indicators (KPIs) and your annual business valuation together. Using your KPIs, react to your benchmarks. Are you achieving your goals? Are you maintaining control? If not, why not? Then change your plan. Do what you must to get back into control.

As you run your business, it's a good idea to review KPIs daily. But now that you're in selling mode, add a monthly meeting to make sure you are making a difference. If things aren't improving the way you expected, update the plan, reorganize your approach, redesign the control points and check back in a month. If things still aren't improving, repeat the process. You will be amazed at the results.

In the next chapters, we'll start forming your 'seller's mindset,' so you approach the sale as wisely as possible.

[9]

Inventory I: Time for a Trip to the Warehouse

IN DOING A DEAL, inventory can cost you the most time, money, headaches, and—if things get emotional—possibly even the most arguments. It may be the biggest dollar value in your sale, so you want to make the most of it.

Inventory can also be an area of low-hanging fruit. Bringing things under control here can have a direct and dramatic impact on the sale price of your business. So let's head out to the warehouse.

TAKE OFF YOUR ROSE-COLORED WAREHOUSE GOGGLES

Begin by taking a good, hard look at your warehouse. Of course *you* know where everything is, but would someone off the street be able to find a product in inventory? Is it well organized?

Consider putting inventory manifests, listing item quantity and location, on the rows. If you are doing official audits of your inventory, have a current one readily available.

Now look down. How does the floor look? It's a common problem: warehouses start out with organized rows and nicely-painted lines. But over time, forklifts wear off the paint and floor plans become re-arranged. So grab some paint cans and update your floor plan.

CYCLE COUNTING AND THE MERITS OF PHYSICAL INVENTORY

How is cycle counting working for you? Businesses that do cycle counting usually claim they are 98% accurate. But a physical count usually turns up less than 90% accuracy.

It's smart to consider doing an old-fashioned, all-day physical inventory. True, it will cost something (approx. $2,000 to verify a $500,000 inventory; get a quote from your accountant). But it's worth the cost. It really brings the skeletons out of the closet.

When doing your inventory, label the following:
· Damaged inventory
· Obsolete inventory
· Inventory on hold for testing
· Old inventory (i.e. over 6 months old)
· Any other category that might devalue inventory

Please understand why this so important. When you take a physical inventory, you are doing two important things:

1. You are verifying that the perpetual number on the books agrees with the physical count

2. You are identifying damaged, obsolete, old (politically correctly called "slow-moving") and questionable inventory. Know this: the buyer is not going to pay for any of it. You might as well have a fire sale on it or discard it.

INVENTORY TIPS FROM THE TRENCHES

Here are some tips to make inventory day go a bit more smoothly:

- Inventory days always start at ridiculously early hours, so show up with donuts.

- There are usually new hires for inventory, so be sure to give very clear instructions. I became famous for threatening that if someone lost a tag, they had to go dumpster-diving to find it. They learned that I was not kidding.

- Make sure you have SOPs or written procedures, so everyone is on the same page. Consistency is crucial here.

- Have two people on each inventory-counting team. This does not mean that the two people count an item at the same time. It means one person follows the other; the second person counts after the first person counts. If two people count together, they tend to get lazy and just go along with the first person's count. If the second team member follows a few minutes after the first person, they have to count it themselves. The main purpose of the team method is to get two separate counts to compare for accuracy.

- Pre-number your inventory tags. Once they are spread all over the warehouse, they're hard to keep track of. You want to make sure none are missing. So pre-number them, and when you hand out the tags, make sure a person signs off for them (i.e. Sam has numbers 20350-20500). At the end of the day, you must account for all used and unused tags.

- Beware of the inventory perfectionist who, in the quest to make everything correct, rips up a tag, throws it away, and rewrites a new one. You'll lose a pre-numbered tag, and lose time looking for it. Don't allow that; insist that procedures be followed to a 't.'

- If you use RF (radio frequency) guns to do inventory, make sure you have enough guns and that they are fully charged. I have seen too many inventories start out using RF guns, but after a while they either don't work or take too long to process. So mid-audit the crew switches to manual count.

- If you are accustomed to using RF guns and are efficient with the process, make sure you have enough computers available and enough individuals to verify the computer data.

THE BEST DAY FOR INVENTORY

Inventory is normally taken on the weekend that is closest to the end of the month. If you are not a 24/7 plant, do it on Saturday. Saturdays are best because you do not want any movement of inventory—no shipments, no deliveries. Especially around the holidays, Saturdays can be difficult, but it really makes sense.

SPECIAL CASE: THE 12/31 INVENTORY

Learn from this true story that happened to me several years ago.

I usually send an email the Monday before year-end inventory, reminding everyone that there will be no shipping/receiving. Unfortunately there are always people who know better, especially on New Year's Eve.

After inventory was finished, I went out to the warehouse. What to my wondering eyes did appear? A truck being unloaded.

Me: "What? I told you no trucks are to be unloaded today!"

Warehouse person: "Yeah, I know. But we were done so I thought it was OK."

Me: "You thought it was OK without asking permission? You are going to mess up the accounting department."

Warehouse person: "Don't worry. I will unload it today and log it in the computer on January 2nd."

Me: "Not a solution! The accounting department is going to receive vendor paperwork that says it was delivered 12/31. They will see it is not in our inventory. If accounting doesn't notice the dates, they will enter it as having been received 12/31. Instant inventory discrepancy. Back on the truck it goes."

This New Year's Eve shenanigan is the oldest vendor trick in the book. Here's how it works:

Although your merchandise is scheduled to be delivered on January 2nd, vendors send the truck out on December 31st so they can log it as a current-year sale on their books. Even if you refuse it, the trucker will still have to drive it back to his company distribution center. Thus he will be on the road, not in the warehouse, when inventory is counted at their end. They will have paperwork proving that it was shipped and sold on 12/31.

As for you, you won't have it on your books, but the inventory resides in the twilight zone. No one owns it.

The point: cut-off dates on inventory can kill you and cause massive errors. If you are dealing with an unhappy or unethical seller or buyer, they may even do these things on purpose if it is to their advantage. So stay on your toes.

HEADS UP INVENTORY WARNINGS

Let me leave you with some final tips to make you as inventory-savvy as possible:

· Pay attention to timing. The valuation must be done on a scheduled date.

- Especially if inventory has been a constant problem in your business, this is the time to clean it up. Future valuation will be much less painful.
- Be especially wary if you have a type of product that employees can walk away with (TVs, computers, etc.).
- Know the loss rate on your inventory. When you compare your physical to book, is the physical count always lower?
- Install cameras in the warehouse to monitor and deter theft.
- Institute documented inventory control measures. These can include receiving and shipping codes of individuals handling inventory.

A hardware/lumber store where I was consulting had a drive-through warehouse to protect product from rain. However, that made it easy for customers to leave the lot with stolen property because no one checked paperwork.

I recommended that they hire a person at the gate to check customer receipts. Because the yard was fenced, it would have been easy for a security person to check the trucks when they left the property.

In the end, the company decided not to hire security because the inventory loss was $2000/month, and it would cost more than that to hire a security person to monitor it.

That may have made sense for them—but if you are selling your business, you may want to hire security to be sure you have inventory controls in place.

In summary, if inventory is a big dollar item on your balance sheet, start paying attention to it now. Make sure your procedures, computer, and inventory numbers are up-to-date and working smoothly. The last thing a buyer wants to hear from an employee is, "This place never had their inventory under control."

Follow Through: Actually Discard What You Write Off

You may think that as long as the books are adjusted after you write off inventory, everything is just fine. If you are fairly presenting the value of your inventory, that is technically true. But leaving it in the warehouse just causes problems, and I don't recommend it.

The biggest problem with writing off inventory and not discarding it: it causes spontaneous generation. No kidding. Somehow the product magically shows up the next time you do a physical inventory—either by people not counting correctly, or by re-counting inventory as good that you said was destroyed or discarded (but wasn't).

This can happen because of personnel changes, or if people forget they wrote it off in the previous month, or even if no one communicates the write-off decision to the warehouse manager. So save yourself a headache and get rid of it.

[10]

Inventory II: What's It Really Worth?

LET'S ASSUME YOU just completed taking the physical quantity of your inventory. Now it is all saleable—no damaged, old, or obsolete items. So how much is it worth?

Why an Audited Inventory is Such a Big Deal

Inventory is probably the biggest dollar value of your deal. The difference between the dollar amount shown on your books and the number calculated after inventory can be very big, and not usually in your favor. This is where the expensive auditor who prepares the information for the sale is worth every penny.

If you're a fairly large company, you're probably already covered because your bank requires an annual audited financial statement. But if you're a smaller company, and all you have is a tax return, then your inventory is not audited. It is worth whatever you, as the owner, say it is.

So why have an audited physical inventory? Because buyers know that inventory is the place where sellers can 'play games.' It's difficult to count. Did you ever try to count fish in a fish tank? They don't stay still for you to count, and neither does inventory. The minute after you take the inventory, forklifts start moving things, and you can't recount it or check for any errors.

The best situation, of course, is for the buyer to be there the day you take inventory. But since several days can pass from the time a seller takes the inventory until a potential buyer visits the plant, an audited inventory adds credibility to the inventory number.

So if you want to sell, better to have audited inventory. A buyer who trusts your audited physical inventory is more likely to give you full value for it.

Using Computer Programs to Calculate Inventory Value

Even if you use a specially-designed computer program, valuing inventory remains a debatable item. There do not seem to be many systems that do this extremely well. Most are passable for raw material and finished goods inventory, which can be proven by market value, invoices, and source documents. But work-in-progress (WIP) has wiggle room—and room for debate. Everything is half-made, half-cooked, or half put together, making it difficult to assign material, labor and overhead.

Many companies simply use what the computer program calculates. That is fine, but be aware that that value is only as good as the person who designed the calculation.

That number is also calculated to satisfy GAAP requirements, which works great for your accountant. But it is a problem when you are considering inventory as part of your business sales price. Why? Because GAAP does not recognize market value. And you want to use market value on your inventory when you sell your business.

So even if you don't have an audited inventory, make sure your numbers make sense.

INVENTORY VALUATION AND WORK-IN-PROGRESS

Let's return to the challenge of valuing work-in-progress. Each business is unique, but I want to give you at least an idea of how it works. Your auditors' experience with this will make them worth their hire.

WIP is a product that is partially made. Picture a car factory that works 7am-3pm, 5 days a week. The whistle blows at 3pm, everyone stops what they are doing and goes home, and we have to assign a value to the partially-manufactured cars.

How do we value a car with a frame, but no body, windows, interior or engine? The answer: it has some raw materials, some labor, and some overhead.

In this simplified example, we would add those components (raw material, labor, overhead) together and assign that value to the WIP. It can get quite complicated when there are many stages of WIP that require different values.

There is a lapse, sometimes up to six weeks, between the time when you take the physical inventory and when negotiations get to the point that you're sharing spreadsheets and inventory dollar amounts. Both parties know that numbers can get a little fuzzy in the interim. Here's an example of the impact that can have on your negotiations.

I was involved in the purchase of a business similar to ours, so I knew what the overhead and raw material figures should be. I also knew how they should be applied to WIP.

Looking at the seller's figures, I insisted that too much overhead was being applied to WIP, causing it to be worth as much as a finished good. Because I knew that the numbers didn't make sense, we negotiated a lower sales price.

If the seller had used an auditor, the numbers would have been more accurate, and I probably would have had more confidence in them.

[11]

Technology:
The Never-Ending Chase

WHAT A PANDORA'S BOX technology opens. It is always changing. The minute you purchase an updated computer or phone, there's a newer one on the market.

Don't Be Stuck in the Past

When selling your business, you don't want to be years behind in technology. Even if you're not up-to-the-minute, at least show that you have a plan for updating, and are in the process of executing it.

Make a Technology Budget

To keep things under control, make a master list of departments and what technology they are due to receive or upgrade each year. Make a budget that rotates areas of your business so that (for instance) every three years crucial equipment is replaced.

TIPS ON BUYING VS. LEASING

The current trend is to lease computers and phones. If you have lease agreements, make sure to have them available to show the buyer. Encourage your CIO (Chief Information Officer) to get lease paperwork organized now to avoid awkward last-minute scrambling. Label each piece of equipment as either 'owned' or 'leased.'

If you lease equipment and your company is large and/or disorganized, be warned. I have seen large companies, in particular, pay serious fees at lease-end because, when it came time to return the products, they were nowhere to be found. Laptops are especially hard to keep track of, with their many chargers and gadgets.

If your company has a high turnover rate of personnel, be prepared to lose things. I repeat, fees charged for lost equipment are astronomical. Consider buying instead of leasing.

TECHNOLOGY AND MERGERS

If you are going to merge your business with another instead of selling outright, save yourself hours of headaches by paying special attention to these details:

· Dates on equipment contracts

· Platforms that each company's equipment uses

· Verify that technology and equipment of both companies can 'talk' to each other

MERGING ACCOUNTING SOFTWARE

This used to be a nightmare, but now it's much easier with consolidation software.

In the past, the accounting department had to determine which company's accounting software would be used, then switch the other company's accounts receivable, accounts payable, inventory, and general ledger to the new software. This meant months of frustration, anger, long hours, retraining, etc.

With consolidation software, there can be a single financial statement and each company can keep its software. The obvious advantage is the ease of transition of the two companies, giving the executive team what they need quickly without forcing both accounting systems to work together.

There are a few drawbacks to consolidation software. If you thought you were going to eliminate personnel by merging accounting systems, and save money with the lowered 'head count,' that is not likely to happen.

If your two companies deliver to the same customer, the customer won't like getting invoices from two different systems. So you may eventually have to merge the two accounting systems. But the urgency is removed, and you can do it at your own pace.

[12]

Evaluating Your Brand

HOW MUCH YOUR BRAND is worth in the sale depends on how good it is. Obviously, the stronger it is, the more it will improve your business's sale price. In fact, your brand might even be what attracted a buyer in the first place.

So first let's discuss how a dollar amount is assigned to the value of your brand. Then we'll explore ways to improve it.

Not a Cut-and-Dried Process

It isn't easy to assign a monetary value to a brand. Most accountants do not value intangible items. And then there are the IRS and GAAP rules. So when assigning a value to your brand, make sure you check with your tax experts when the sell is in the final negotiating stage.

Branding and goodwill are often considered together for valuation, and simply labeled 'goodwill.' The value of goodwill can't be proven by invoices, bills of sale, and appraisals; it is a subjective number.

To fix a value, ask these questions: is the brand/goodwill value attributable to the quality of the product? Great customer service?

Brand strength? All of the above? In your sale negotiation, everyone at the table will have an opinion—especially you.

There really isn't a mathematical formula to put a price on branding, but that is to your advantage when you are selling. If you are a good salesperson and a good negotiator, make the most of it that you can.

In the end, the deciding factor will simply be whatever the buyer will agree to. So put your best brand image out there now, and be a tough negotiator when the time comes.

Assignment of Goodwill

The concept of 'goodwill' began in 1920 and hasn't left us since.

Asset-based business valuation requires that, after a value is assigned to all assets, the difference between the selling price and the assigned assets is 'goodwill.' The buyer will want to assign higher value to inventory, fixed and tangible assets, and less to goodwill. As seller, you will want to place an accurate value on inventory, fixed and tangible assets, with the remainder of your asking price allocated to goodwill.

Both the buyer and seller must agree to the assignment of selling price at settlement, so this will be another area where your accountant will be very valuable to you.

Make sure you get both legal and tax advice on this point because the tax treatment of goodwill may look different to you and the seller. But if you do what is fair, and document your reasons for the value you assign to goodwill, you will probably be fine.

Building Value into Your Brand

Take a good, objective look at your brand. You can be sure prospective buyers will. Is it recognizable and strong? Remember, your brand is more than just your name. It's your promise of excellence to the marketplace.

The goal is for your prospective buyer to know your brand is a powerhouse because people trust it. And that is worth money in the bank at sale time.

BUILDING VALUE INTO YOUR NAME

You may think your company's name is set in stone, but it is worth at least putting it through the 'strong name test.' Strong names are memorable and almost always simple. If you have a weak name, and you have three to five years to establish equity in a new one, you may be better off changing it now.

BUILDING VALUE INTO YOUR LOGO

Now take a look at your logo. A great logo is instantly recognizable, and not cute, slick or trendy. If you have a cliché, or 'logo-ish' design, or if it makes your company look like it was founded in 1973 (even if it was), consider freshening it.

BUILDING VALUE INTO YOUR TAGLINE

A tagline works great as a positioning statement. Taglines that are specific, short, and pithy get remembered. Try to avoid worn out terms like 'quality,' 'best,' 'service,' 'excellence,' 'solution,' etc. Taglines benefit from being changed every few years; maybe now is a good time.

BUILDING VALUE INTO YOUR WEBSITE

Your website will probably be the source of introduction for your prospective buyer—and first impressions are indelible.

To make your business look as valuable as possible, your website should be clean, open, and up-to-date in design, content, and code. It should support your brand and generate a steady stream of sales and/or leads. To do that, it must be user-friendly and benefits-focused.

Your buyer will want to inspect your Google Analytics and AdWords accounts, so learn to use your most effective keywords or hire someone to do it for you.

The design of your website can only go as far as your branding graphics will allow—it's tough to design a beautiful website around a logo that looks like it's stuck in the 1970s. So pay close attention to both. As with your brand identity, hire the best web designer you can afford. Money invested here can reap a great ROI.

Good Design is Worth the Investment

In my experience, when you are selling a business, attraction is key. And attraction starts with your logo and your brand. Sure, it may end with the numbers, but brand is where it all begins.

Malcolm Forbes famously said that corporate image is the single most leverageable investment a company can make. Good design is a competitive advantage, and strong branding can increase the perceived value of your company. Coca-Cola® is a classic example of brand value. It is said that the Coca-Cola brand is worth more than all of its other assets combined.

So if you are serious about rebranding, don't be pennywise and pound foolish. Find an experienced designer who specializes in corporate identity and branding. He or she will be able to advise whether you should rebrand entirely, or merely freshen your logo while retaining as much brand equity as possible. Just as you would with your lawyer or accountant, hire the best advice you can afford.

[13]

Your Management Team

A REAL BUSINESS can run itself without you. You know that, right?

The right buyer wants to buy a well-run business. A well-run business needs a strong management team. So strong that it can run without you.

Not sure if your business can run without you? Here are a few test questions:

1. Are you typically the only one making major decisions on a daily basis?

2. When you go on vacation, can you relax? Or are you constantly on the phone micromanaging?

3. Is the need to control and micromanage in your DNA? Have you taken a DISC® test to learn your strengths and weaknesses in this area? (DISC® is a popular personality assessment tool. The acronym stands for dominance, inducement, submission and compliance.)

If the answers to these questions leave you feeling sheepish, making some changes will help smooth the transfer of power.

RIGHT PEOPLE, RIGHT POSITIONS, RIGHT NOW?

Your buyer will want to know your assessment of the staff, so be ready to give an honest answer.

Certainly, you hope your HR department hired all the right people in the first place. (If not, it's tempting to toss blame in their direction. But that isn't going to fix your personnel problems quickly, so don't go there just yet.)

If HR did hire quality people, you still have questions to ask. Your company hasn't been stagnant—things happen all the time that cause people to move to different positions, for which they may or may not be well suited.

So, how to find out if employees are where they belong? It may sound counterintuitive, but the best way to find out if everyone is where they should be is to learn how they got where they are now. If they've moved up the ladder, what was the reason for the promotion? Were they qualified? Were they fully trained? How's their new track record?

WHO STAYS, WHO GOES?

Your buyer may ask your opinion of who you would keep, and who you would let go, if you were them. So give it some thought ahead of time.

Is there someone who just doesn't fit in? For instance, you may have a highly-skilled maintenance engineer who has been promoted to department manager, although he does not like people. Be on the lookout for the Peter Principle in action.

You know where this question is going next – if you have key executives who are under-performing, why haven't you let them go already? Individuals are often promoted because of their relationship with the owner or years-in-service, not because of their management capabilities. Now is the time to clean house and align capabilities.

(If you haven't read Jim Collins' book, *Good to Great*, this is a good time to order it and learn how to be sure you have the right people on the bus ASAP.)

On a memorable first day on the job, I was asked to fire a sweet 65-year-old lady who had been with the company for 30 years. I told them I wouldn't do it until I had assessed the individual and documented her performance review. Management was unhappy, but I stuck to my guns.

She left a year later, but everything was documented as to her job performance, and she was now ready to retire. She left with dignity and respect.

My opinion: if a non-performing employee has been with a company for 30 years, management bears responsibility for having allowed it to continue for so long.

Lesson: Although it's tough to be objective, remember that your opinion as to whether a person is a great employee may differ from the opinion of the individuals buying your company.

THE VALUE OF AN UP-TO-DATE ORGANIZATION CHART

Although they're falling out of popularity, organization charts are crucial in buying, selling, and merging companies. This is especially true in the early stages when the purchase or merger is confidential and you can't talk directly to your employees.

If you don't have one, there are Word templates and software to guide you through the process. I have seen organization charts that fold across a conference table, and subsets of charts that look like a puzzle. That's not necessary here. All you need at this point are the key management positions.

> *On a job interview, my prospective employer pulled out an organization chart to show me where I'd fit in the company. As he reviewed it with me, he crossed out positions that had been eliminated and people who were no longer with the company. By the time he was finished, there were so many boxes crossed out that I decided not to take the job.*

YOUR VERY OWN A-TEAM

Who is on your executive management team? All the C's, plus a few key players:

- CEO (Chief Executive Officer)
- CFO (Chief Financial Officer)
- COO (Chief Operations Officer)
- Quality Manager
- Human Resource manager

Other possibilities, depending on your product or service:

- CIO (Chief Information Officer)
- Sales Manager
- Plant Manager
- Safety
- Marketing
- Public Relations

I recommend no more than 10 individuals at your team meetings or efficiency will suffer and you won't get done within an hour.

Your buyer will ask—so make sure you have an up-to-date folder on each of your key executive staff members, including the following contents:

· a biography
· signed employment contracts including:
  length of contract
  covenants not to compete
  sales commissions
  bonus structure
  base salary

YOUR MANAGEMENT TEAM IN ACTION

Whether your business is service, retail, or manufacturing, your management team needs to learn to work together for the good of your business, especially under pressure.

For example, here's how a good management team might work in a plant:

Say there's a major employee issue. You call everyone on the management team to a meeting. Everyone.

You might think it should just be the CEO, COO, and HR manager. But it's smarter to call in everyone on the executive team, even if the CFO and QM aren't going to contribute to the decision-making. That way they all know the facts and the truth when rumors start spreading. All team members called, all bases covered.

Now imagine there's a defective product in the field. As is your habit, you assemble the whole team. Each one contributes something important. Your CFO remembers to call the insurance company within 24 hours of the incident. Your HR manager inventories who was in house and out-of-house, if the defect was caused by one particular employee. QM helps diagnose if employees were properly trained to detect defects and follow SOPs. Together they decide what a solution will cost.

SHARING FINANCIAL INFORMATION WITH YOUR TEAM

It's tempting to keep all numbers close to your vest. But it's much smarter to share important parts of both financial and non-financial data that your managers need to make decisions in their departments.

If you don't already, start scheduling weekly and monthly profit reviews with your team. Even if it takes time for them to learn accounting terminology, they'll discover that every decision and action in your plant has a financial consequence.

When working with a dog food factory, I needed a way to get the management team interested in unit cost figures. Noticing that the owners and plant managers frequently had unlabeled cans in their hand, I made a label that showed all the unit cost figures on it. I made eight of them, and handed them out at the next financial meeting.

Soon, management starting asking questions like, "If I have the maintenance department work overtime this weekend, how will that affect the unit cost?" The inventory manager asked me, "How much would it cost to take inventory on a monthly basis? Is it worth it?" The whole company benefitted from these lines of questioning at our financial meetings.

TRANSITION: BUMPY OR SMOOTH

The transition can be smooth or difficult, depending on your management style. If you've always treated everyone like family, your management team may feel abandoned, rejected, and hurt when they find out that you've sold the business. Involving them with the purchase may help them feel more valued and cause the transition to be more successful.

Team Building and Transition Coaching

Is your management team a congenial, well-oiled machine? If not, do research to find some of the great team-building exercises available.

Consider hiring a transition team coach to teach your team the skill sets necessary to deal with the changes ahead. This is often overlooked because owners don't feel it is necessary, or don't want to spend money in this final phase of the transition. But if you've ever dealt with an unhappy employee, you know it saps hours of time from you and anyone sitting close to them in the office.

So spend the money on transition coach experts. It may not work for everyone on your management team, but if the majority is 'on board,' the transition will be much smoother.

An added bonus: a stronger team sense will minimize employee turnover.

Budget an off-site team-building day into your transition costs. It can really pay off. I know of a company that did a team building exercise two weeks before the different companies' employees started working together. It was great because the first day on the job everyone already knew each other on a personal, fun level before they got down to work.

Merging Management

If you're considering merging companies instead of selling outright, be warned. Merging management is typically one of the most misunderstood (and least prepared-for) parts of the transition. Be ready for it, and you'll be way ahead of the game.

The people structuring and pricing your deal will look for synergies and economies of scale.

Where's the first place they look? In management. No need for two CFOs, two HR managers, two QMs. So much money can be saved.

This may be true, but it's not as simple as it sounds. Each CFO uses different accounting software systems, so it's not so easy to get rid of the second CFO. To keep him or her, they rename the position controller or assistant CFO. No savings there.

Next up: HR managers. No need for two of those, right? But now there are twice as many employees—too much payroll and benefits work for one person. So they rename the second HR position and split payroll and benefits into two jobs. So much for cost savings and synergy.

MANAGING MANAGEMENT DURING THE TRANSITION

How you handle management can make the difference between a successful or unsuccessful transition.

If you've ever tried to do a project with uncooperative people, you know it takes twice as long and becomes a painful memory of a horrible experience. So go for the buy-in.

The more you keep your team informed during the process, the more likely they will willingly help with transition tasks.

It may help to require management to read the classic book, *Who Moved My Cheese?* Encourage understanding that it's not that the way things were done previously was wrong . . . they were just done differently from what you'll do going forward.

Transition: If You're Selling Internally

If you've been training someone for the CEO position, it often works well to name that position Executive Vice President. It is a signal to everyone in the company that this person is going to take over when you leave. And it will do one of two things: either (1) give your employees comfort because they know the business will continue and who will be at the helm, or (2) give them a heads-up opportunity to get out if they don't like the person in charge.

I once heard that at Bethlehem Steel, whenever the president retired to Chairman of the Board, they gave him an office in the Hotel Bethlehem so he wasn't in the corporate office and placed him on so many boards that he didn't have enough time to get involved in corporate matters. I don't know if this is true, but I do know Mr. Martin had an office in Hotel Bethlehem . . .

Transition: If You're Selling Externally

Many times the new owner will be the CEO, and will ask you (now the 'previous owner'), to stay on as an employee during a transition period. The compensation and hours are normally outlined in the purchase agreement.

Sometimes this works out, and the new owner appreciates your wealth of knowledge.

Other times, the new owner will want to make changes, and this will be difficult to do with the old owner (you) present. Therefore the transition period is often cut short, but the compensation to you is continued.

If you already have a sustainability plan in place, and your management team can run the company while you go golfing, you already know that the company can run properly with the new owner.

[14]

Know Your Buyers: Are They Inside or Outside the Company?

YOU CAN BE SURE of one thing: whoever your buyer is, they will be either inside or outside of your company.

INSIDE: SUCCESSION AND SUSTAINABILITY

If your buyer is inside your company, they are members of your executive staff, or family members, or both. You will want to be prepared for the challenges of these inside-the-business buyers.

First, understand that the way businesses move to the next generation has changed in recent decades.

Privately-held businesses used to be owned primarily by one family and passed on from generation to generation. The main concern was simply a smooth passing of the baton.

Today it is more common for businesses to sell to executive staff rather than family members.

The benefits are win-win all around.

Employees who are buying the business become more dedicated, interested, and motivated. Whether they are buying all or part of the business, they will tend to make growth and improvement-oriented decisions. Financial sustainability of the company becomes a healthy focus.

If you choose to go this route, you will face a roadblock: your employees may require help to make the purchase. Since financing has become more difficult, and fewer individuals have ready investment cash, there is a growing popularity of 'earn-ins' and 'earn-outs.'

EARN-INS AND EARN-OUTS

One popular method of an 'earn-in' is simply to pay your employees enough salary or compensation so they can afford to buy shares.

With an 'earn-out,' buyers and sellers can tie the purchase price to the future success of the business. To you, as seller, this has the advantage of allowing you to remain involved in the business and the disadvantage of not allowing you to make a clean break.

To the buying employees, the upside of the 'earn-out' is that, if the business declines after purchase, both seller (you) and buyer share in the decrease in funds.

No matter which method your employees use, it is important for everyone to focus on the sustainability of the business. Will the product or service be needed and desired in the future? All parties will be interested in this, and in keeping up with innovation and technology.

I cannot overstress the value of sustainability planning, especially if you are considering selling to your employees. It takes a different kind of thinking, and stands in contrast to the typical focus on quarterly dividends, personal payroll agenda, and the short-sightedness of taxes.

Instead, the future owners are future-oriented. They care that the business is green and sustainable for the environment. They work to continue supplying jobs for their employees. They will find ways to be remain profitable. Quality, production, process, and price will constantly and consistently be monitored.

The good news is that success will come with sustainability, because failure will not be an option. A remarkably forward-thinking way of operating, it will be the new culture of cutting edge businesses.

Whether you sell to your employees or keep it within the family, there will be challenges. For instance, if you sell within the family, there are many regulations on gift tax and capital gains to consider. So be sure you understand the whole picture. And always make sure you check with your tax accountant before making any final decisions.

Outside: From Soup to Nuts

If selling your business to insiders sounds too complicated, selling outside the company has its own challenges.

YOU: THE ONE-MAN SHOW

One common problem occurs when your buyer is unfamiliar with your business or product, and/or you are the only one that knows the inner workings of your company.

Points are deducted on your business valuation when you, the one owner-manager, are exiting the company along with all the business knowledge. Buyers understandably fear that, for instance, you are the only one that knows a major customer only pays every 60 days and will bail if the new owner changes their terms.

You can head this problem off by starting now to delegate and share the wealth of knowledge you've accumulated.

BABY-BOOMERS
Doug Hepburn, CPA, PFS, CFP, says "...with 7 million companies owned by Boomers and 10,000 Americans turning 65 every day, the volume of small businesses changing hands is expected to achieve historic proportions." Fall 2012 PA CPA Journal.

There are a lot of baby boomers entering and exiting the small business market; some of them might be your prospective buyers.

Boomers that have owned a business for 35 – 40 years are ready to get out (that might be you).

But there are others who are finished with corporate life, but want to keep working. Frustrated after decades in a Dilbert cube, they think that if only they could be the one running the business, everything would be different. But they have no business-ownership experience. This mindset reminds me of childless couples who say, "If I were their parent, that kid would listen to me!"

These can be good buyers, but keep your eyes and ears open, and be careful what you wish for.

COMPETITORS AND CUSTOMERS
There are two more outside groups that might want to buy your business.

A competitor would typically want to buy your business because they want to shut down the competition.

During negotiations, they will promise that they won't shut down the plant, and your loyal employees will not lose their jobs. Many honor that agreement for a year or two, but then shut down your plant because their larger plant can handle the volume. If your situation fits this model, and you don't like what you see in the tea leaves, beware.

Customers may want to purchase your company for vertical integration. They hope that, if they buy a supplier, they'll produce the product for low cost, therefore reducing their cost to produce at the next level. If the numbers work for both of you, this can be a win-win deal.

Some say that you can expect competitors and customers to make you the best offers. Just remember: they are used to negotiating and are usually shrewd business dealers. So beware of the sharks.

Bonus Points: Negotiate a Consulting Fee for Yourself

Here's an often-overlooked reward for the knowledge you've accumulated all these years. Whether you are selling inside or outside of your company, if you are going to help with the transition, negotiate for a consulting fee.

The beauty of a consulting fee is that you come in just when they need you, for help with a client or a scheduled meeting. Contracts can require up to 40 hours a week, but it is completely up to you how you negotiate this section of the deal.

As difficult as it may be (or not), remember that it is generally best for all involved if you hand the reins over to the new owners, and only visit the office when scheduled or invited.

Wondering what to do if negotiations aren't going so well? See page 105 or download "Red Flags and Deal Breakers: 10 Signals That You Should Not Go Through With the Sell" at www.ForWhatItsReallyWorth.com.

[15]

Partial Sell: When You Don't Want to Sell it All

IN CHAPTER 14, we discussed selling your business to an 'inside' buyer—an employee of your company. I pointed out that they rarely have enough cash to buy 100%.

ESOP MAKES IT POSSIBLE

Welcome to the world of ESOPs: Employee Stock Ownership Plans.

People who work for corporations can get stock as bonuses, or they can buy it. ESOPs are often part of employee benefit packages and, until lately, weren't available to small businesses. But now small- and medium-sized companies are beginning to use ESOPs as a vehicle for employees to own parts of the company.

If you are a 'C' or 'S' corporation, this method may be an option for you. But you need to know ahead of time that it's complicated. The thumbnail version: you sell your stock to the ESOP, then the ESOP plan designates shares to your employees. Check with your tax and legal advisors to see if this is a good option for you. A good reference is *Selling Your Business to an ESOP* (see the Appendix).

Shark Tank: Trade Partial Ownership for Cash

If you've ever watched the TV show *Shark Tank*, you already know that a partial sell can be a very good idea.

Here's how it works. You believe strongly in the future prospects of your product or service. But you need an infusion of cash for inventory, equipment, marketing, etc.

You find a buyer who is willing to invest. But since nothing in life is free, you have to give up part of your business in exchange. For this to work, both you and the buyer have to believe strongly that you will turn a good profit.

The advantage to a partial sell: you get an immediate cash infusion and can set about improving your business. If you have maxed out your personal cash, your line of credit and your credit cards, this can be a solution for you.

The disadvantage: If you are looking to withdraw from your business, you haven't exactly sold it. You're still tied to it, and you still have to worry about it at night. You're headed in the right direction, but the process can be slow. But in a tough economy, you might not have another choice.

If you are a long-range planner, or if your kids will be taking over the business in five years, a partial sell may make sense for you.

Sometimes the numbers work, and sometimes they don't. If you go to www.ForWhatItsReallyWorth.com, you will find our **Partial Sell Calculator** interactive spreadsheet. Play with it to see how much money you can receive, depending on what percentage of ownership you are willing to sacrifice.

16

If Your Business is Sinking: How to Sell the Titanic

IF YOU OWN a business as large as the Titanic, the world says you are "too big to fail, or go to jail."

But what if you're a small business, and you have that sinking feeling? I urge you to consider selling instead of closing your business.

In the last few years, I've watched a lot of small businesses in our local market just shut down, without even trying to sell. I think this is a mistake. There is almost always a better way out.

YOU ALWAYS HAVE SOMETHING TO SELL

Despite how discouraged you are, consider this: you always have something to sell. Your book of customers. Your name. Your location. A chandelier. There is always something.

Let's say you have a yacht-sized business and the underwater obstacles loom large. There is no more capital, no more loans. Both your accountant and your banker say you can't continue.

They may be correct, but telling you to close your doors instead of selling is wrong. If you can wrangle even six more months, here is what you can do.

Right away, reach out to a management accountant. Ask them to examine your selling price and expenses. Give them (and yourself) a finite period of time, such as six months, to turn your business around, and possibly prepare it to be sold.

Then contact a lawyer and/or accountant who does business valuations. They may also know of potential buyers and can help you negotiate a deal to sell your business. Depending on how connected you are with other individuals in your type of business, you may just have to put out the word that you are 'thinking' of selling, and someone may come knocking at your door.

Using a business broker is another possibility, but I suggest you explore the other avenues first. Like selling your own home, if you can find your own buyer you can save the broker fees. If you do hire a broker, be sure to structure an arrangement that they get paid at the time of the sale.

Your bank will work with you in this process. It's in their best interest because they are more likely to get their money back if you sell instead of close or go bankrupt.

And Speaking of Your Banker . . .

Is your banker in the lifeboat with you? They should be, because if you go down, they go down with you.

So if you're taking on water, don't wait for your banker to call you—call them first. Please don't let your pride get in the way. Maybe it is a little embarrassing to say you need help, but the consequences of not communicating with your banker are worse than making that call. So pick up the phone.

You are likely to find out that your banker actually wants to work with you. They are as interested in your success as you are – they do not want to run your business or sell it.

I hear bankers say things like, "If they had only reached out or called sooner, I would have worked with them on payment terms." One thing they can do is to switch your line of credit, which can be called at any time, into a term loan. Then you can have a fixed rate for a longer term, with a smaller monthly payment.

If you can show the bank that you have a solid business plan, they are usually willing to give you that six months you need.

You Will Weather the Storm

Sometimes you can come out ahead; sometimes you can break even. But most of the time you will come out of it in one piece, not being in debt and still owning your home.

Coming out in one piece sure beats sinking, doesn't it? I'm sure the Titanic passengers would have thought so.

17

The Pot of Money You Need to Sell Your Business

DON'T BE LIKE the person who hopes to sell their business tomorrow just by announcing that it's for sale. If you want a healthy return, you're going to have to do more than just put up a 'For Sale' sign.

INVEST IN YOUR SELL

Instead, invest in your sell. Planning ahead for these expenses will reduce unpleasant surprises and put you in a healthier negotiating position.

Nearly any business will sell if the price is lowered enough. But if you want a decent return on your blood, sweat, and tears, you need to prepare. Selling your company will be emotional enough. Don't add the trauma of getting less than you thought it was worth.

Just like home appraisers add value for finished basements and subtract value for old bathrooms, so do prospective business buyers. Sure, you can sell with old accounts receivables and ancient inventory. But the buyers are just going to make deductions to your selling price.

So how much are you going to have to spend?

A good starting point is 10% of the value of your business. That means you shouldn't be surprised if you have to spend $50,000 to sell a $500,000 business.

For that amount, you will hopefully get most or all of the following:

· appraisal of your business
· business valuation
· audit of your inventory

Your building spruce-up usually costs about 10% of the value of the building.

Additional items you may need proposals for:

· branding
· website

Selling fees: If you plan to use a broker, you are responsible to pay the fee (typically about 7%).

· For a $1 million business, the fee would be $70,000
· For a $100,000 business, expect to pay a flat fee of $7,000.

Advisors:

· Best practice is to put together a trusted team of advisors. Set aside the cost for four advisors for one year. Keep them on retainer for scheduled meetings, with unlimited support phone calls.

· Expect to pay about $7200 annually for each of the four advisors, total cost $28,800.

· Instead of choking on this number, think of it as cheap insurance. It will save you money in the long run – and possibly even save you from disaster.

SEVERANCE PAY

The first thing to say about severance and retention bonuses: they can add up to a sizeable amount. Make sure you are getting a large enough selling price to cover the amount you expected plus this amount. If you don't, it will be coming out of your profit on the sale of the business.

Severance pay can be as simple as an additional paycheck or as complicated as a detailed severance package.

Severance rules are very complicated, and they vary widely depending upon the size and structure of your business. It is very important that you get advice from a lawyer that specializes in labor and employment law and a tax accountant who is familiar with the severance tax laws.

Once you've gotten that expert advice and decided what you're going to offer, calculate the dollar amounts and set aside that money.

TYPICAL SCENARIOS

Severance is often calculated as a week's pay for every year of service, although this provision is more common when companies are shutting down than when they are being sold.

If you are terminating some employees during the sale or merger, it's common to offer severance pay and possibly health benefits for a specific period of time. I have seen some employers be very generous with severance pay, possibly because it relieves some guilt over selling the business. Others do the bare minimum required by law.

In an earlier chapter we discussed the importance of knowing the contracts of your top executives. Do any of their contracts contain severance packages? Look carefully. The reason they are called packages is that they often include health benefits, bonuses, resume help, career training, counseling, and out-placement assistance for a fixed period of time (usually six months).

PAY-TO-STAY: RETENTION BONUSES

Once the rumor is out that your company is being sold or merged, you can expect some employees to run for the hills.

To prevent this from happening, and to discourage employees from leaving before the merger is complete, you can offer pay-to-stay bonuses.

Retention bonuses are appropriate when you're selling your business. They are usually offered only to key employees or employees that have a special skill that is difficult to replace.

You can be selective on who is offered a retention bonus, but check with HR law and your tax accountant first. You should also discuss this topic when you discuss which employees and positions you want to retain after the sale or merger.

MISCELLANEOUS EXPENSES

It's a smart idea to set aside money for a team-building day for your management team to help the transition go smoothly.

Because each business is unique, you will probably have thought of costs specific to your own company. Add them to your list.

"SHIRTSLEEVES TO SHIRTSLEEVES IN THREE GENERATIONS"

I remember one owner of a three-generation business who thought the $50 million he was being offered sounded like such a huge sum. He assumed it would be sufficient to pay off his loans and still leave enough cash for retirement. But when all was said and done, the cost of severance and retention bonuses and the many other expenses involved in selling his business ate up all of the remaining cash. He had nothing left but lack of indebtedness.

Have you heard the old proverb, "shirtsleeves to shirtsleeves in three generations"? The first generation rolls up its sleeves and builds the business with hard labor. The second generation enjoys the profits and benefits, but doesn't continue building. The third generation has no experience with real work, so it either consumes the family fortune or rolls up its sleeves and again returns to hard labor.

Especially if you're the third generation of a family business, I sincerely hope the advice in this book helps you disprove the proverb.

[18]

The Dance of the Deal™
and How to Keep it Moving

LEARN THE CAREFULLY choreographed steps in the deal process. This is a fairly typical scenario; if you're lucky, it will take about six months. Your actual deal may take more or less time.

January 1   **SELLER: Putting it out there**

You have a price, you selected a broker. You listed your business on www.bizbuysell.com. You wait for a bite.

February 1   **BUYER: Inquiring**

Buyer has done their homework. They know what kind of business they wish to buy, the location, how much they can spend. They make an inquiry.

SELLER: Giving location and one-sheet financials

You disclose the location and the Buyer Listing Report with one-sheet financials. You wait to see if the buyer is still interested.

March 1   **BUYER: Further requests**

Buyer determines that the location and financial sheet is within their parameters. They now request 5-year-past financials, tax returns and audit reports.

March 7   **SELLER: Intent**

You request that the potential buyer sign a confidentiality agreement, put 20% down, and sign a Letter of Intent to purchase the business.

BUYER: Counter

Buyer signs the confidentiality agreement and offers to put 10% down with their Intent to Purchase agreement.

March 15   **SELLER: Letter of intent signed**

You agree to 15% down, sign the Intent to Purchase agreement, and give the potential buyer the financial statements as requested.

BUYER: More research

Buyer gives the financial information to their accountants to do their own valuation calculation and decide on a price they feel the business is worth.

ACCOUNTANT: Calculation

The buyer's accountant determines that their calculated price is within range of the seller's asking price.

April 1   **BUYER: Request to visit business**

May 1   **SELLER: Request date for settlement**

BUYER: Due diligence

Buyer contacts their lawyer and accountant for their due diligence list. The search for skeletons begins in earnest.

SELLER: Near compliance

You supply most of the information on the buyer's list and deliver the information. If printed, the pile of documents stands a foot high.

BUYER: Negotiation continues

Buyer lists and requests missing information, while continuing negotiation. They also enlist their own real estate appraisal and send their COO (and operations employees) to inspect machinery and equipment. They send in an auditor to verify physical inventory and the value of inventory.

> *NOTE: This whole process is done confidentially. Therefore it is always difficult to send non-employees into the company for inspection without raising eyebrows.*

BUYER: Price validation

Buyer now has all the information necessary to determine if your price is valid.

Inventory — Buyer notes that the inventory is overvalued and some inventory is obsolete and damaged. They deduct for obsolete and damaged inventory.

Accounts receivable — Buyer determines that some accounts receivable are old. They deduct old accounts receivable and set a dollar amount to be held in escrow.

Reappraisal — Buyer's real estate appraisal comes in lower than yours, and financing will only approve buyer's number. Buyer deducts for decreased real estate value.

Machinery and equipment — Buyer's operations employees discover that machinery is old and not well-maintained. The operations manager gives a new value for machinery and equipment. Buyer deducts the decreased value in machinery and equipment.

June 1   **BUYER: Makes a counteroffer**

SELLER: Counteroffer received

You decide to accept, reject, or counter the offer.

June 3   **SELLER: Accepts the deal**

(or, more likely, goes back and forth three, four, or five more times)

You accept the counteroffer, settlement is scheduled, final agreements are signed, and announcements are made.

June 30   **SETTLEMENT**

Remember, any case studies, examples, stories or illustrations cannot guarantee that you will achieve similar results. Factors such as your market, personal effort, and other circumstances may and will cause results to vary. In fact, your results may vary significantly.

How to Keep the Dance Moving

As you see from "The 'Dance of the Deal," questions and answers go back and forth during the process, and they can drag things out for months.

If you find this happening to you, make sure your buyer is (1) serious, and (2) not dragging it out on purpose. Yes, due diligence takes time. But be sharp and stay on top of it.

Quick Response is Key

What can you do to keep the sale from dragging on?

Most importantly, respond quickly to all communications concerning the sale. That includes you, your executive team, and your outside advisors. Since your legal and tax advisors have other clients to serve, if you don't stay on top of things, they may not. So keep an eye on everyone involved, making sure they respond immediately to all emails and requests for documentation.

This will require a lot of oversight on your part (it may even feel like babysitting), but you must do it to keep things moving forward. The easiest way for a buyer to delay the purchase is to say, "You didn't answer my email," or, "You didn't give me the information I wanted."

Buyer Motivations for Feet Dragging

Remember, you don't know what is happening on the buyer's side. Maybe they're having a hard time getting financing. Maybe they see the economy, interest rates, or the stock market moving in a direction that favors delay. All the more reason for you to keep things moving forward.

Don't Let Extraneous Promises Affect the Dance

Depending on your original motive for selling, you may have promised your spouse you would be in Florida before the first snowfall. Or maybe you promised the bank that the loans would be paid off by October. Your children may be expecting their slice of the pie as a Christmas present.

The pressure to deliver on these promises may make you settle for less, which would be tragic after all the work you did to increase your sales price.

So remember, **don't make promises!**

Stay In Control

Your best bet is to stay in control of the process until you get up from the settlement table. Remember the Plan-Organize-Control-Feedback loop, and keep the sale moving.

I've learned that if negotiations last over six months, the deal has a 50-50 chance of happening. If the deal goes over a year, it is probably never going to happen. Keep it moving, and this won't happen to you.

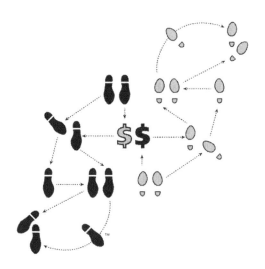

[19]

A Graceful Exit

THERE'S AN ART to leaving with grace. Preparing yourself ahead of time will help you be your best self, all the way through to the settlement table.

RUMORS ARE FLYING

You marketed and found a buyer for your business. In the process, lots of questions were asked. Mysterious phone calls were made behind closed doors. Strange people showed up at the plant. Rumors are everywhere. Maybe it's time to spill the beans.

The announcement to your employees should be handled delicately.

AVOIDING THE MASS EXIT

Your company is the means of support for most of your employees. If they fear they are going to lose their job, they may start looking for another one immediately.

Knowing this, many companies that are preparing to sell or announce a shutdown give bonuses to employees who remain through the transition. It even has a name: the 'pay-to-stay' bonus. These bonuses are usually fairly substantial—as much as it takes to convince many to stay on board. Hopefully, you have set enough money aside to encourage retention.

Don't Blow the Big Announcement

Imagine your company is about to engage in a merger. Knowing that you want to handle the announcement properly, you schedule an early-morning meeting the next day for the employees. All owners and managers plan to visit each plant to break the news simultaneously. You have prepared Q&A sheets and a carefully-worded press release.

After everyone goes home at 6pm, you email the press release to the newspaper, figuring it will be in the next morning's news. Big mistake.

By 7pm the information is on the newspaper's website. Friends and relatives of your employees are calling them in alarm. Almost everyone has the news before you have a chance to unveil the official announcement.

Although you will insist, "We were going to tell you first," until you are hoarse, it won't matter. The employees are furious with management. Lesson learned.

It's Time to Hand Over the Keys

So you've told the employees, and by-and-large they stuck with you. You made it through settlement. You have cash in your pocket and you got what you wanted.

Right?

Take a deep breath and remember that morning you woke up and decided to sell your business. You wanted free time. To retire. To get on with your life, whatever that means to you.

It has been a tiring and stressful six months. But it is over now. Sometimes it's good to just "take the money and run." Try not to look back.

No Seller's Remorse Allowed

Remember the last time you bought a car? You had such a challenge trying to decide which make, model, and color to buy. You finally made up your mind—and by the time you got home you thought you should have bought 'the other one.'

Don't do that. Don't doubt yourself. You made and worked your plan. You surrounded yourself with experts. You followed all the directions. You are ready to enjoy the fruits of your labor.

So make a new list—your bucket list. And start checking things off.

See you at the beach.

❧

12 Interview Questions to Ask Your Team of Professional Advisors

These interview questions will help you choose members for your team of trusted advisors. It's important to gauge the amount of experience each person has, and if they were actively involved in the details of deals or simply provided oversight.

1. Approximately how many mergers, acquisitions, buying or selling deals have you been involved in over your career?

2. How many deals were you involved in within the past year?

3. How long (in months or years) did the last several deals take?

4. How much time (in hours) did you spend on the last several deals?

5. For a fairly recent deal similar to mine, were you involved in designing the deal?

    a. Did you help set the selling price?

    b. Did you help design the compensation package?

    c. Were there delays beyond your control?

    d. Were you instrumental in shortening the deal length?

    e. Were you involved in the financing?

    f. Were you involved in negotiating?

6. If you were included in setting the selling price, did you do the business valuation? Did you review a business valuation prepared by someone else?

7. Did you supply the information to recast the financial statements for the business valuation?

8. Were you involved in gathering and/or reading all of the documentation for due diligence?

9. Were you involved with the personnel and organizational phase of the sale?

10. Did you prepare the organizational chart?

11. What was your favorite part of the selling process?

12. What phase of the selling process did you not enjoy?

Please email 3 to 5 references to us.

Printable versions (PDFs) of these documents are waiting for you at www.ForWhatItsReallyWorth.com.

Red Flags and Deal Breakers:
10 Signals that You Should Not
Go Through With the Sell

Stay clear-headed and be ready to pull the plug on the deal if you receive any of these negative signals:

1. The buyer's deposit check bounces.

2. The bank rejects the buyer's loan request to buy the business. (Make sure you know this early on.)

3. You don't think your employees will get along with the new management (listen to your intuition).

4. You aren't getting the dollar amount you honestly feel you deserve. Come to terms with this before you sign any papers.

5. The buyers send signals that they aren't going to maintain the quality and reputation that you've worked so hard to build.

6. You hear rumors that the buyer is going to shut down the business after they buy it.

7. The buyer keeps changing the details of the buy-sell agreement.

8. There have been too many downward revisions (e.g., lowered value of inventory, lowered accounts receivable, reduced value of branding) and you have compromised too much. Having a 'walkaway number' in mind before you begin negotiations will help you know if you've reached this trigger point.)

9. It is taking too long to agree upon a settlement date.

10. You discover the buyer has lied to you.

Suggested Reading List and Bibliography

Andrew Carnegie
David Nasaw, New York: Penguin, 2006

The E-myth Revisited: Why Most Small Businesses Don't Work and What to Do about It
Michael E. Gerber, New York: CollinsBusiness, 1995

Fish!: A Remarkable Way to Boost Morale and Improve Results
Stephen C. Lundin, Harry Paul, and John Christensen. New York: Hyperion, 2000

Good to Great: Why Some Companies Make the Leap—and Others Don't
James C. Collins, New York: HarperBusiness, 2001

Selling Your Business to an ESOP (9th Edition)
Keith Apton, Michael Coffey, Ronald Gilbert, Joseph Rafferty, Loren Rodgers, Corey Rosen, Kenneth Serwinski, Brian Snarr; Oakland, CA: The National Center for Employee Ownership, 2012

Who Moved My Cheese?
Spencer Johnson, New York: G P Putnam, 1998

Links to Online Documents

To download the helpful documents referenced in this book, please visit www.ForWhatItsReallyWorth.com.

Printable PDFs:

The Dance of the Deal

12 Interview Questions for Your Team of Professional Advisors

Red Flags and Deal Breakers: 10 Signals That You Should Not Go Through With the Sell

Suggested Reading List and Bibliography

Interactive spreadsheets:

Business Selling Timeline: A powerful spreadsheet for you to list and track the activities involved in selling your business. Use it to plan and adjust dates based on duration and delays. Share the plan with your team during your weekly status meetings.

Partial-Sell Calculator: In the heat of negotiations, it's not always easy to translate a buy-in offer into actual dollars. This spreadsheet will help you quickly determine how much the buyer is saying your business is worth to them, so you can compare it to your own figure.

ABOUT THE AUTHOR

Gerry T. Pandaleon, CPA, CMA, FCPA, brings three decades of experience as a CPA, controller, and CFO to this user-friendly guide to selling your business.

Readers can trust Gerry's from-the-trenches advice on how to prepare their businesses for sale. The same clear, no-nonsense communication style that leads to success for her clients will help you avoid costly mistakes and walk away from the settlement table a happy person.

Gerry's consulting and CFO-sharing practice focuses on the growth of small- to mid-size companies that range from $15 to $150 million in sales, with 60 to 120 employees. She especially enjoys teaching clients how to read their financial statements and use key performance indicators. She is future-focused, constantly looking for ways to improve clients' businesses.

Having worked extensively with service, retail, and manufacturing businesses (such as packaging, bottling, and meat processing), Gerry is highly qualified to help companies understand both their financial and non-financial data, to make and reach their goals. Her CMA and FCPA (Forensic Certified Public Accountant) training allows her to pinpoint constraints, restructure and investigate financial records, and do the analysis needed for future planning.

Gerry has travelled nationally and internationally, including two years spent in Taiwan working with KMPG. A natural teacher, she serves as adjunct professor for a local university and community college. She has two grown children and lives in Bethlehem, Pennsylvania, with her attorney husband.

Look for Gerry's next book, *How to Buy a Business for What It's Really Worth*.

Made in the USA
Charleston, SC
22 July 2013